Adopting Pets with Confidence

A Comprehensive Guide to Choosing and Caring for Your New Friend

Angelica Romero

1

Adopting Pets with Confidence

clarifying purposes only and are owned by the owners themselves, not affiliated with this document.

Table of Contents

Chapter 1: Preparing for Pet Adoption

Understanding the Adoption Process

Understanding the adoption process is a crucial step for anyone considering bringing a new pet into their home. This journey can be both exciting and overwhelming, but having a clear understanding of each stage will ensure a smoother experience. The process involves several key steps: researching, applying, visiting, and finally, adopting. Each of these stages requires careful consideration and preparation.

Research is the foundation of a successful adoption. Start by exploring the types of pets that align with your lifestyle. Consider factors such as the size of your living space, your activity level, and any allergies. Some people might thrive with a high-energy dog, while others may prefer the quiet companionship of a cat. Additionally, consider the time you can dedicate to a pet. Puppies and kittens require more attention and training, while older animals might be more independent.

Once you have an idea of the type of pet you're interested in, it's important to research different adoption sources. Shelters, rescue groups, and reputable breeders each offer unique options. Shelters often have a variety of animals and focus on rehoming pets in need. Rescue groups may specialize in specific breeds or types of animals, providing a more tailored experience. Reputable breeders, on the other hand, can offer insights into specific breeds and their characteristics. Each option has its advantages, so take time to consider which aligns best with your values and lifestyle.

The application process is the next step and can vary depending on where you choose to adopt. Shelters and rescues often require potential adopters to fill out detailed applications. These forms typically ask about your living situation, previous pet experience, and your plans for the new pet's care. Be honest and thorough in your responses. The goal is to ensure a good match between you and the animal. Some organizations may also conduct home visits to verify that the environment is suitable for a pet.

Visiting potential pets is an essential part of the process. This is your opportunity to meet different animals and observe their behaviors firsthand. Spend time interacting with them to understand their personalities. Some may be shy at first, while others might be more immediately affectionate. Pay attention to how they respond to you and any family members present. It's also helpful to ask the shelter or rescue staff about the animal's history and any known health issues. This information can offer valuable insights into the pet's needs and temperament.

Making the decision to adopt is both exciting and nerve-wracking. It's important to trust your instincts and consider how the pet will fit into your life long-term. Reflect on the interactions you had during your visit and discuss any concerns with the adoption staff. They can provide additional guidance and help address any uncertainties. Remember, adopting a pet is a lifelong commitment, and it's crucial to feel confident in your choice.

The adoption day itself is filled with anticipation. Before bringing your new pet home, ensure you have all necessary supplies ready. This includes food, bedding, toys, and any required medications. Familiarize yourself with the pet's routine and dietary needs. Having everything prepared in advance will make the transition smoother for both you and your new companion.

After the adoption is finalized, many organizations offer resources to support you and your pet. These can include training classes, veterinary services, and behavioral consultations. Take advantage of these opportunities to build a strong foundation for your relationship. Ongoing support can help address any challenges that arise and ensure a successful integration into your home.

Understanding the adoption process is more than just following steps; it's about preparing for a lifelong partnership. By investing time and effort into each stage, you're setting the stage for a rewarding and fulfilling journey with your new pet. Embrace the experience with an open heart and mind, and you'll be well-equipped to provide a loving home for your new family member.

Assessing Your Readiness for a Pet

Assessing your readiness for a pet is a crucial step in the journey toward responsible pet ownership. Bringing a pet into your home is a long-term commitment that requires careful consideration of your lifestyle, resources, and emotional preparedness. This chapter will guide you through the key factors to evaluate before making the decision to adopt.

First, consider your lifestyle and daily routine. Pets, much like people, thrive on consistency and attention. Dogs often require regular walks, playtime, and social interaction, while cats might need less direct supervision but still benefit from engagement and affection. Think about your work schedule, travel habits, and social life. If you're frequently away from home or working long hours, you might need to plan for pet care services or reconsider the timing of your adoption.

Financial readiness is another critical aspect. Pets come with both initial and ongoing expenses. The initial costs can include adoption fees, vaccinations, spaying or neutering, and basic supplies like food dishes, bedding, and toys. Ongoing expenses often involve regular veterinary check-ups, grooming, food, and unexpected medical costs. It's wise to create a budget and consider whether your current financial situation can comfortably support these expenses. Remember, a pet is a long-term financial commitment, potentially spanning 10 to 20 years.

Your living situation plays a significant role in determining the type of pet that might be suitable for you. Consider the size of your home and whether you have a yard or access to outdoor spaces. Apartments can be great for smaller pets or certain cat breeds, while a larger dog might thrive in a house with a backyard. Additionally, check any pet-related restrictions if you're renting. Some leases have limitations on pet types, sizes, or breeds.

It's also essential to reflect on your family dynamics. If you live with others, whether it's family, roommates, or a partner, it's important that everyone is on board with the idea of bringing a pet into the home. Discuss responsibilities and expectations to ensure that everyone is prepared to contribute to the pet's care. If there are young children or elderly family members, consider the pet's temperament and energy level to ensure a harmonious match.

Your emotional readiness is just as important as practical considerations. Pets require patience, love, and attention. They can be a source of immense joy but also demand emotional investment, especially during training phases or if health issues arise. Assess your current emotional state and whether you're ready to welcome the ups and downs that accompany pet ownership. Pets often sense and react to their owners' emotions, so being in a stable place emotionally can benefit both you and your pet.

Understanding the time commitment involved is vital. Puppies and kittens, for example, require significant training and socialization to grow into well-behaved adults. This involves time and patience for activities like house training, obedience lessons, and social outings. Even older pets need regular interaction and engagement to ensure they remain happy and healthy. Reflect on whether you're prepared to dedicate this time regularly.

Consider your motivation for wanting a pet. Are you looking for companionship, a running buddy, or perhaps a family pet to teach your children responsibility? Understanding your reasons can help guide you to the right type of pet and ensure your expectations align with reality. Pets are not just temporary solutions for loneliness or boredom; they are lifelong friends who depend on you for their well-being.

Lastly, think about future plans and potential lifestyle changes. Are you planning to move, start a family, or change careers? Such changes can impact your ability to care for a pet. Try to anticipate any significant life events that might affect your pet's stability and care. Being prepared for these changes can help you make a more informed decision.

Ultimately, assessing your readiness for a pet is about making an informed, thoughtful decision that considers both your needs and the well-being of the animal. It's a process that requires honesty and careful planning, ensuring that when you do welcome a pet into your home, it's a positive experience for both of you. Taking the time to evaluate these factors not only benefits you but also ensures a loving and stable home for your future pet.

Setting Expectations and Goals

Setting expectations and goals is a fundamental part of preparing for pet ownership. As you embark on this journey, it's crucial to establish what you hope to achieve and how you plan to integrate your new companion into your life. This process will help ensure a harmonious relationship and set the stage for a fulfilling experience for both you and your pet.

Begin by reflecting on your motivations for adopting a pet. Are you looking for companionship, a playful addition to your family, or perhaps a partner for outdoor activities? Understanding your primary reasons can help shape realistic expectations. Acknowledging these motivations will guide you in selecting a pet that aligns with your lifestyle and emotional needs.

Once you have a clear understanding of your motivations, consider the specific characteristics you desire in a pet. This might include energy levels, temperament, size, or grooming requirements. For instance, if you're an active person, a dog with high energy might be a perfect match. Conversely, if you prefer a quieter lifestyle, a calm cat or an older dog might suit your home better. Setting these expectations upfront will help you find a pet that fits seamlessly into your daily routine.

It's essential to establish realistic goals for your relationship with your pet. Training is often a significant part of pet ownership, especially with younger animals. Consider what you want to achieve in terms of obedience, socialization, and behavior. Whether it's teaching basic commands or ensuring your pet is comfortable around strangers, setting clear training goals will provide structure and direction. Patience and consistency are key, as each pet will learn at their own pace.

Another important aspect is to define what a successful integration looks like for your household. Think about how your pet will fit into your family dynamics. If you have children, involve them in setting expectations and responsibilities. This not only helps with training but also fosters a sense of shared ownership and accountability. Discuss how daily routines might change and ensure everyone is prepared to adapt to the new member of the family.

Consider the socialization goals for your pet. Exposure to different environments, people, and other animals can greatly influence your pet's behavior and confidence. Plan outings and interactions that will help your pet become well-adjusted and comfortable in various settings. This is particularly important for dogs, who often thrive on social interaction. Remember, gradual exposure and positive reinforcement can ease the process and build your pet's confidence.

Health and wellness should also be key components of your expectations and goals. Regular veterinary care, a balanced diet, and exercise are essential for a pet's well-being. Set goals for maintaining your pet's health, such as scheduling routine check-ups and vaccinations. Consider any specific health needs your pet might have, particularly if you're adopting a breed known for certain medical conditions. Being proactive about health can prevent issues and ensure a long, happy life for your pet.

As you set these goals and expectations, remember that flexibility is crucial. Pets, like people, have unique personalities and may not always meet your expectations. Be open to adapting your goals as you learn more about your pet's individual needs and preferences. This adaptability will help foster a strong bond built on understanding and mutual respect.

Financial planning is another important aspect when setting expectations. Outline a budget that covers not just the basics like food and grooming but also unforeseen expenses such as emergency vet visits. Understanding the financial commitment involved will prevent surprises and allow you to provide the best care for your pet.

Finally, envision the long-term future with your pet. Consider how your life might change over the years and how your pet will fit into those changes. Whether it's moving to a new home, starting a family, or changing careers, having a pet is a long-term commitment. Planning for these eventualities will help ensure that your pet remains a cherished part of your life through all its stages.

By carefully setting expectations and goals, you lay the groundwork for a rewarding journey with your pet. This thoughtful approach ensures that both you and your pet thrive in a loving, supportive environment, creating a bond that will last a lifetime.

Budgeting for Your New Companion

Budgeting for your new companion requires careful planning and foresight. Bringing a pet into your life is a joyful experience, but it's also a financial commitment that can span many years. Understanding the costs involved and preparing accordingly will ensure you can provide the best care for your furry friend.

Start by considering the initial expenses. These often include adoption fees, which can vary depending on the type and breed of the pet. Shelters and rescue organizations usually charge less than breeders, but it's important to research and choose a reputable source regardless of the cost. Additionally, you'll need to budget for vaccinations, spaying or neutering, and microchipping. These essential medical procedures are crucial for your pet's health and safety.

Beyond these initial medical expenses, you'll need to invest in basic supplies. These include food bowls, collars, leashes, and ID tags. Creating a comfortable environment with a cozy bed, toys, and scratching posts or chew toys is also important. Don't forget about grooming supplies, such as brushes or nail clippers, especially if your pet requires regular grooming.

Food is a significant ongoing expense. The cost can vary widely based on the size of your pet and any specific dietary needs. High-quality food is an investment in your pet's health, potentially saving money on vet bills in the long run. Consider buying in bulk or subscribing to a delivery service to reduce costs.

Routine veterinary care is another important factor. Regular check-ups, vaccinations, and dental care are essential to keeping your pet healthy. It's wise to set aside funds for annual visits and any additional treatments that might arise. Pet insurance is an option that can help manage unexpected medical expenses. Research different plans to find one that fits your budget and your pet's needs.

Unexpected medical emergencies can happen at any time. Setting up an emergency fund specifically for your pet can provide peace of mind. Even a small monthly contribution can build up over time, ensuring you're prepared for any unforeseen expenses.

Training and socialization are often overlooked but vital components of your pet's well-being. Depending on the type of pet, you may need to budget for obedience classes or professional training services. These are particularly beneficial for dogs, helping to build a strong bond and ensuring good behavior.

Pet care services such as boarding or pet-sitting should also be considered, especially if you travel frequently. Research local options and their costs, and plan for occasional use. Alternatively, you might rely on friends or family, but having a professional service as a backup is always a good idea.

Grooming can be a significant expense, especially for breeds with specific grooming needs. Regular visits to a professional groomer might be necessary, or you may choose to learn how to groom your pet yourself. Investing in good-quality grooming tools can save money over time.

Consider any specific needs your pet might have based on their breed or age. Some breeds are prone to certain health issues, which might require special diets or regular treatments. Older pets might need more frequent veterinary visits or medications. Understanding these potential costs ahead of time will help you budget more accurately.

If you're adding a pet to a family with children, factor in any additional costs for child-pet interaction training or safety measures. These might include gates or pet-proofing supplies to ensure a safe environment for both your children and your pet.

Finally, think about the long-term costs associated with pet ownership. As pets age, they may require more medical attention or special accommodations. Planning for these eventualities will help you manage your budget effectively over the years.

By taking a comprehensive approach to budgeting, you'll ensure that you can provide a loving and stable home for your new companion. Understanding these financial commitments and planning accordingly will allow you to enjoy the companionship and joy a pet brings without unexpected financial stress.

Researching Breeds and Species

Researching breeds and species is a crucial step in finding the perfect pet to fit your lifestyle. With countless options available, it's important to understand the characteristics and needs of different animals to ensure a harmonious match. This chapter will guide you through the process, helping you make an informed decision that benefits both you and your future companion.

Begin by reflecting on your lifestyle and environment. Consider factors such as your living space, daily routine, and activity level. For example, if you live in a small apartment, a large, energetic dog might not be the best choice. Instead, a smaller breed or a cat could be more suitable. Understanding your environment will help narrow down the options and focus your research on breeds or species that align with your circumstances.

Next, think about the time and commitment you can realistically offer. Some pets require significant attention and interaction, while others are more independent. Dogs typically need daily exercise, training, and socialization, whereas cats may be content with less hands-on time. Exotic pets, like reptiles or birds, might have unique care requirements that demand specialized knowledge. Honest self-assessment at this stage is crucial to avoid future mismatches.

Once you have a clear idea of your lifestyle and time availability, delve into the specific traits of different breeds or species. Dogs, for instance, come in a vast array of breeds, each with distinct characteristics. Some breeds are known for their intelligence and trainability, like Border Collies or Golden Retrievers, while others may be more stubborn or independent. Similarly, cats also vary widely; Siamese cats are known for their vocal nature, whereas British Shorthairs are typically more reserved.

Consider the health predispositions of different breeds. Some are prone to specific genetic conditions that could lead to higher veterinary costs and care requirements. Research these aspects thoroughly to prepare for any potential challenges. For example, Bulldogs often face respiratory issues due to their brachycephalic nature, while large breeds like Great Danes may be susceptible to joint problems.

Social needs are another important factor. Some animals thrive on interaction and companionship, both from humans and other animals. If you're frequently away from home, consider a pet that is more independent or think about adopting two animals to keep each other company. Dogs are generally more social, requiring regular interaction, while certain cat breeds or small mammals might be content with less frequent engagement.

Dietary needs and feeding habits also vary among breeds and species. Understanding these requirements is essential for providing proper nutrition and maintaining health. Some pets may have specific dietary needs due to their breed, age, or health conditions. Researching these aspects will ensure you meet their nutritional needs from the start.

Grooming requirements can differ significantly and should be factored into your decision. Long-haired breeds, whether cats or dogs, often need regular grooming to prevent matting and maintain cleanliness. This could mean frequent visits to a professional groomer or learning to manage grooming at home.

If you prefer low-maintenance pets, look for breeds with shorter coats or those that require minimal grooming.

Energy levels and exercise needs are crucial when choosing a pet. High-energy dogs, like Huskies or Jack Russell Terriers, need ample exercise and mental stimulation, while a Basset Hound or a Persian cat may be more relaxed. Matching your pet's energy level with your activity level is key to a happy coexistence.

Training and intelligence can vary greatly among breeds and species. Some dogs, like Poodles and German Shepherds, are highly trainable and eager to learn, while others may require more patience and persistence. Consider your willingness and ability to invest time in training, as this will impact your choice.

Finally, consider the lifespan of the pet you're interested in. Some animals, like parrots and tortoises, can live for decades, requiring a long-term commitment. Understanding the potential lifespan will help you prepare for the years ahead.

By thoroughly researching breeds and species, you can find a pet that complements your lifestyle and brings joy and companionship into your life. This careful consideration ensures a lasting and fulfilling relationship with your new companion.

Chapter 2: Finding the Right Pet

Choosing Between Shelters and Breeders

Choosing between shelters and breeders is a significant decision when welcoming a new pet into your life. Each option offers unique benefits and challenges, and understanding these can help you make an informed choice that aligns with your values and lifestyle.

Imagine walking into a shelter, surrounded by hopeful eyes and wagging tails. Shelters are filled with animals seeking a second chance, often rescued from difficult circumstances. Adopting from a shelter is not only a compassionate choice but also an opportunity to provide a loving home to an animal in need. Many shelters perform thorough health checks, vaccinations, and spaying or neutering procedures before adoption, ensuring your new pet is ready for a fresh start.

A common misconception about shelter animals is that they are all troubled or unhealthy. In reality, many are surrendered due to changes in their owners' lives, such as moving or financial difficulties. These animals are often well-behaved and simply in need of a stable environment. By adopting from a shelter, you contribute to reducing overpopulation and supporting organizations that work tirelessly to care for homeless animals.

On the other hand, breeders offer the chance to choose specific breeds with particular traits and temperaments. If you have your heart set on a specific breed due to its characteristics, a reputable breeder might be the right option. Breeders can provide detailed information about lineage, health histories, and breed-specific needs, helping you understand what to expect as your pet grows.

When considering a breeder, it's crucial to prioritize ethical practices. Reputable breeders prioritize the health and well-being of their animals, providing clean environments, socialization, and proper care. They should be transparent about health screenings and willing to answer any questions you have. Visiting the breeder's facility can provide insights into the conditions the animals are raised in and the level of care they receive.

Contrastingly, puppy mills and unethical breeders prioritize profit over animal welfare, often resulting in poor living conditions and health issues. Recognizing the signs of a responsible breeder is essential. Look for breeders who limit the number of litters per year, allow you to meet the mother and siblings, and provide a nurturing environment.

Cost is another factor to consider. Adopting from a shelter is generally more affordable, with adoption fees covering basic medical procedures. Breeders typically charge higher prices, reflecting the costs of maintaining breeding programs, health screenings, and care. While the initial investment may be higher, understanding the long-term financial commitment is vital for either choice.

Personal stories often illuminate the impact of these decisions. Consider Sarah, who adopted a mixed-breed dog from a shelter. Initially hesitant about the dog's background, she discovered a loyal companion who quickly adapted to her home. The bond they formed was enriched by knowing she had given her dog a second chance at happiness.

Conversely, Mark chose a Labrador Retriever from a breeder, drawn to the breed's friendly nature and compatibility with his active lifestyle. By selecting a breeder committed to health and temperament, he found a pet that seamlessly fit into his family, providing years of joyful companionship.

Both experiences highlight the importance of aligning your choice with your expectations and lifestyle. Whether you choose a shelter or a breeder, patience and research are key. Spend time getting to know the animal, understanding its needs, and ensuring it matches your living situation.

Consider the long-term implications of your choice. Shelter animals may come with unknown histories, requiring patience and training. Breeder animals may have specific health needs based on their breed. Both require commitment and care, and neither choice is inherently superior. What matters most is the dedication to providing a loving and stable home.

Ultimately, choosing between shelters and breeders depends on your priorities, lifestyle, and the qualities you seek in a pet. Both paths offer the joy of companionship and the satisfaction of adding a beloved member to your family. By making a thoughtful decision, you set the foundation for a rewarding and lasting relationship with your new companion.

2.2   Visiting   Shelters: What   to   Look   For

Stepping into an animal shelter can be an overwhelming experience, filled with the cacophony of barking dogs and the hopeful gazes of cats peering through their enclosures. For many, the decision to adopt a pet is driven by a desire to provide a loving home to an animal in need. However, the process of selecting the right shelter and understanding what to look for can be daunting. This chapter delves into the essential aspects to consider when visiting shelters, ensuring that your adoption journey is both rewarding and informed.

The first impression of a shelter often sets the tone for the entire adoption process. Cleanliness is paramount; a well-maintained facility not only reflects the shelter's commitment to animal welfare but also ensures the health and safety of its inhabitants. As you walk through the doors, take note of the overall environment. Are the floors clean? Is there a noticeable odor? While some level of animal scent is inevitable, a strong, unpleasant smell may indicate inadequate sanitation practices. The enclosures should be tidy, with fresh bedding and clean water readily available for the animals.

Staff interaction is another critical factor. The demeanor and knowledge of the shelter staff can greatly influence your experience. Friendly, approachable staff members who are willing to answer questions and provide guidance are invaluable. They should be knowledgeable about the animals in their care, able to provide insights into each animal's personality, health history, and any special needs. This information is crucial in helping you make an informed decision about which pet might be the best fit for your home.

Observe the animals themselves. Healthy animals typically have bright eyes, clean coats, and exhibit normal behavior for their species. Dogs may wag their tails and approach the front of their kennels, while cats might be curious and playful. Be cautious of animals that appear lethargic, have discharge from their eyes or nose, or exhibit signs of distress. While some animals may be shy or anxious due to the shelter environment, these physical symptoms could indicate underlying health issues.

The shelter's adoption process is another aspect to consider. A reputable shelter will have a thorough adoption procedure in place, designed to ensure that animals are placed in suitable homes. This process often includes an application, an interview, and sometimes a home visit. While it may seem rigorous, these steps are in place to protect both the animal and the adopter, ensuring a successful match. Be wary of shelters that have minimal requirements or seem eager to expedite the adoption process without proper vetting.

Inquire about the shelter's policies on spaying and neutering. Responsible shelters will ensure that all animals are spayed or neutered before adoption, or will require adopters to commit to having the procedure done. This practice is crucial in controlling the pet population and preventing the birth of unwanted animals. Additionally, ask about the shelter's return policy. Life circumstances can change, and a reputable shelter will have a policy in place that allows adopters to return animals if necessary, ensuring that the pet is cared for regardless of the situation.

Consider the shelter's resources and programs. Many shelters offer post-adoption support, such as training classes, veterinary care, or behavioral consultations. These resources can be invaluable, particularly for first-time pet owners or those adopting animals with special needs. Shelters that invest in these programs demonstrate a commitment to the long-term welfare of their animals and the success of their adoptions.

The shelter's transparency is also a key consideration. Reputable shelters will be open about their operations, including their funding sources, adoption statistics, and euthanasia rates. This transparency reflects their accountability and dedication to ethical practices. If a shelter is hesitant to provide this information, it may be a red flag.

Finally, trust your instincts. The adoption process is as much about finding the right shelter as it is about finding the right pet. If something feels off or if you have concerns about the shelter's practices, don't hesitate to explore other options. There are many shelters and rescue organizations, each with its own approach and philosophy. Taking the time to find a shelter that aligns with your values and expectations will enhance your adoption experience and increase the likelihood of a successful match.

Visiting shelters is a crucial step in the adoption journey, offering a glimpse into the lives of animals waiting for their forever homes. By paying attention to cleanliness, staff interaction, animal health, adoption processes, and shelter policies, you can make an informed decision that benefits both you and your future pet. The right shelter will not only provide a safe haven for animals but also support you in your quest to offer a loving home to a deserving pet.

Understanding Animal Temperaments

Understanding animal temperaments is a vital aspect of the adoption process, as it helps ensure a harmonious relationship between the pet and its new family. Each animal, much like humans, possesses a unique personality shaped by genetics, environment, and experiences. Recognizing these traits can guide potential adopters in selecting a pet that aligns with their lifestyle and expectations.

The concept of temperament encompasses various behavioral traits, including sociability, energy levels, adaptability, and response to stress. Observing these characteristics in a shelter setting can be challenging, as the environment may not reflect the animal's true nature. However, with patience and keen observation, one can glean valuable insights into an animal's temperament.

Sociability is a key component of temperament, influencing how an animal interacts with humans and other animals. Some pets are naturally outgoing, eager to greet new people and make friends. These animals often thrive in bustling households with frequent visitors. Conversely, more reserved animals may prefer quieter environments and require time to warm up to new acquaintances. Understanding an animal's sociability can help determine whether it will be comfortable in your home.

Energy levels vary widely among animals and can significantly impact daily life. High-energy pets, such as certain breeds of dogs, require ample exercise and mental stimulation to prevent boredom and destructive behavior. These animals are well-suited for active families who enjoy outdoor activities and have the time to engage in regular play sessions. On the other hand, low-energy pets may be content with leisurely walks and quiet companionship, making them ideal for individuals with a more relaxed lifestyle.

Adaptability refers to an animal's ability to adjust to new environments and routines. Some pets are highly adaptable, quickly settling into new homes and embracing changes with ease. These animals are often more resilient to disruptions, such as moving or schedule changes. Less adaptable animals may struggle with transitions, requiring a stable and predictable environment to feel secure. Assessing an animal's adaptability can help ensure a smoother transition into your home.

Response to stress is another crucial aspect of temperament. Animals, like humans, experience stress, and their reactions can vary widely. Some pets remain calm and composed in stressful situations, while others may become anxious or fearful. Understanding how an animal copes with stress can inform your approach to training and socialization, as well as help you create a supportive environment that minimizes stressors.

To accurately assess an animal's temperament, it's essential to spend time observing and interacting with them in various settings. Engage with the animal in a quiet space, away from the noise and distractions of the shelter. This allows you to observe their natural behavior and gauge their comfort level. Pay attention to body language, vocalizations, and reactions to stimuli, as these can provide valuable clues about their temperament.

Consulting with shelter staff can also offer insights into an animal's temperament. Staff members often have firsthand experience with the animals and can share observations about their behavior and preferences. They may also provide information about the animal's history, which can shed light on any past experiences that may have shaped their temperament.

It's important to remember that temperament is not fixed and can evolve over time. With patience, training, and positive reinforcement, many animals can overcome behavioral challenges and develop new traits. For example, a shy animal may become more confident with socialization and exposure to new experiences. Similarly, a high-energy pet can learn to channel its energy into constructive activities with proper guidance.

When considering an animal's temperament, it's crucial to reflect on your own lifestyle and expectations. Are you seeking a companion for outdoor adventures, or do you prefer a pet that enjoys quiet evenings at home? Do you have the time and resources to support a pet with special needs or behavioral challenges? By aligning your expectations with an animal's temperament, you can foster a fulfilling and lasting relationship.

Understanding animal temperaments is a nuanced process that requires observation, patience, and empathy. By taking the time to assess an animal's sociability, energy levels, adaptability, and response to stress, you can make an informed decision that benefits both you and your future pet. This thoughtful approach not only enhances the adoption experience but also lays the foundation for a harmonious and rewarding companionship.

2.4   The   Importance   of   Meeting   Multiple   Pets

Meeting multiple pets before making an adoption decision is a crucial step in finding the right companion for your home. Each animal has its own unique personality, and what might seem like a perfect match on paper could turn out differently in person. By interacting with several animals, you increase the likelihood of finding a pet whose temperament, energy level, and needs align with your lifestyle.

The process of meeting multiple pets begins with an open mind and a willingness to explore different possibilities. It's easy to become enamored with a particular breed or appearance, but focusing solely on these aspects can lead to overlooking the deeper connection that forms the foundation of a successful adoption. Instead, consider the qualities that are most important to you in a pet, such as sociability, playfulness, or calmness, and use these criteria to guide your interactions.

When visiting a shelter or rescue organization, take the time to observe the animals in their environment. Watch how they interact with staff, volunteers, and other animals. This can provide valuable insights into their social skills and comfort levels. Some pets may be more reserved in a shelter setting due to the unfamiliar surroundings, while others may be more outgoing and eager to engage. By observing these behaviors, you can begin to identify which animals might be a good fit for your home.

Engaging with multiple pets allows you to experience a range of personalities and behaviors. Spend time with each animal individually, allowing them to approach you at their own pace. This can help you gauge their level of interest and comfort in your presence. Pay attention to body language, such as wagging tails, relaxed postures, or avoidance behaviors, as these can indicate how the animal is feeling.

During these interactions, consider how each pet's energy level matches your own. A high-energy dog may be perfect for someone who enjoys outdoor activities and has the time to provide regular exercise, while a more laid-back cat might be ideal for a quieter household. By meeting multiple pets, you can better assess which energy level complements your lifestyle.

It's also important to consider the pet's adaptability to your home environment. Some animals may have specific needs or preferences, such as a quiet space to retreat to or a fenced yard for play. Discuss these considerations with shelter staff, who can provide valuable insights into each pet's history and any special requirements they may have.

Meeting multiple pets can also help you identify any potential behavioral challenges that may arise. For example, a dog that is overly excitable or a cat that is particularly shy may require additional training or socialization. By recognizing these traits early on, you can make an informed decision about whether you have the resources and commitment to address these needs.

In addition to observing and interacting with the animals, take the opportunity to ask questions about their backgrounds and any known medical or behavioral issues. Understanding an animal's history can provide context for their behavior and help you anticipate any challenges that may arise. Shelter staff and volunteers are often well-acquainted with the animals in their care and can offer valuable insights into their personalities and needs.

As you meet multiple pets, it's essential to remain patient and open to the possibility that the right match may not be immediately apparent. Building a connection with an animal takes time, and it's important to trust your instincts when evaluating each interaction. Sometimes, the bond you form with a pet may be unexpected, but it can lead to a rewarding and fulfilling relationship.

Once you've had the opportunity to meet several animals, take some time to reflect on your experiences. Consider which interactions felt the most natural and which pets seemed to resonate with you on a deeper level. This reflection can help you make a thoughtful and informed decision about which pet is the best fit for your home.

Meeting multiple pets is a valuable step in the adoption process, allowing you to explore a variety of personalities and behaviors. By taking the time to engage with different animals, you increase the likelihood of finding a companion that truly complements your lifestyle and needs. This thoughtful approach not only enhances the adoption experience but also lays the foundation for a successful and lasting relationship with your new pet.

Making the Final Decision

Deciding to bring a new pet into your home is a significant commitment that requires careful consideration and thoughtful deliberation. The final decision is not merely about choosing an animal that appeals to you aesthetically or emotionally; it involves evaluating various factors to ensure a harmonious and lasting relationship. This chapter delves into the essential aspects to consider when making the final decision, providing practical guidance for prospective pet owners.

The first step in making the final decision is to assess your lifestyle and living situation. Consider your daily routine, work schedule, and social commitments. A pet requires time, attention, and care, and it's crucial to determine whether you can accommodate these needs. For instance, a dog may need regular walks and playtime, while a cat might be more independent but still require companionship and stimulation.

Reflect on whether you have the time and energy to meet these demands consistently.

Your living environment also plays a significant role in the decision-making process. Evaluate the size and layout of your home, as well as any outdoor space available. Some pets, like large dogs, may thrive in a spacious environment with a yard, while others, such as small rodents or reptiles, may be perfectly content in a more confined space. Additionally, consider any restrictions imposed by landlords or homeowners' associations regarding pet ownership.

Financial considerations are another critical aspect of the decision. Owning a pet involves ongoing expenses, including food, veterinary care, grooming, and supplies. It's essential to create a budget and ensure that you can comfortably afford these costs without compromising your financial stability. Unexpected expenses, such as emergency veterinary care, should also be factored into your financial planning.

Once you've assessed your lifestyle, living situation, and financial readiness, it's time to reflect on your personal preferences and expectations. Consider the qualities you desire in a pet, such as temperament, energy level, and size. Think about how these traits align with your personality and lifestyle. For example, if you enjoy outdoor activities and have an active lifestyle, a high-energy dog might be a suitable match. Conversely, if you prefer a quieter, more relaxed environment, a calm and independent cat could be a better fit.

It's also important to consider any potential challenges or limitations you may face as a pet owner. Allergies, for instance, can significantly impact your ability to care for certain animals. If you or a family member has allergies, research hypoallergenic breeds or species that may be more suitable. Additionally, consider any physical limitations or health conditions that may affect your ability to care for a pet. Be honest with yourself about your capabilities and seek a pet that aligns with your abilities.

The decision-making process should also involve input from other members of your household. If you live with family or roommates, discuss the responsibilities and expectations associated with pet ownership. Ensure that everyone is on board with the decision and willing to contribute to the care and well-being of the pet. This collaborative approach helps prevent misunderstandings and ensures a supportive environment for the new addition.

Once you've considered these factors, it's time to revisit the pets you've met during your search. Reflect on your interactions and the connections you felt with each animal. Trust your instincts and consider which pet resonated with you on a deeper level. Sometimes, the right choice may not be the one you initially expected, but rather the one that feels most natural and comfortable.

Before making the final decision, it's advisable to spend additional time with the pet you're considering. Arrange for a trial visit or foster period if possible, allowing you to observe the pet's behavior in your home environment. This experience can provide valuable insights into how the pet adapts to your lifestyle and whether any unforeseen challenges arise.

As you approach the final decision, it's essential to remain patient and open-minded. The right pet may not come along immediately, and it's important to resist the urge to rush the process. Take the time to ensure that your choice is well-informed and aligned with your long-term goals and expectations.

Once you've made your decision, prepare your home for the new arrival. Gather the necessary supplies, such as food, bedding, toys, and grooming tools. Create a safe and comfortable space for the pet to acclimate to their new environment. Establish a routine that incorporates feeding, exercise, and bonding time, helping the pet feel secure and welcomed.

The final decision to adopt a pet is a profound and life-changing choice that requires careful consideration and thoughtful planning. By evaluating your lifestyle, living situation, financial readiness, and personal preferences, you can make an informed decision that leads to a fulfilling and harmonious relationship with your new companion. Embrace the journey with an open heart and a commitment to providing a loving and nurturing home for your pet.

Adoption Day: What to Expect

Adoption day is a momentous occasion, filled with anticipation, excitement, and a touch of nervousness. It's the day when you officially welcome a new member into your family, marking the beginning of a shared journey. Understanding what to expect on this day can help ease any anxieties and ensure a smooth transition for both you and your new pet.

The first step in preparing for adoption day is to confirm all necessary arrangements with the adoption agency or shelter.

Ensure that you have completed any required paperwork and that you understand the adoption process. This may include providing identification, proof of residence, or references. Clarifying these details in advance can prevent any last-minute surprises and allow you to focus on the joy of the occasion.

On the day of adoption, it's important to arrive at the shelter or adoption center with a sense of calm and readiness. Bring along any required documents and identification, as well as a carrier or leash, depending on the type of pet you are adopting. Having these items on hand demonstrates your preparedness and commitment to providing a safe and secure environment for your new companion.

As you enter the adoption center, take a moment to absorb the atmosphere. Shelters can be bustling places, filled with the sounds of animals and the chatter of staff and visitors. It's natural to feel a mix of emotions, from excitement to empathy for the animals still awaiting homes. Allow yourself to experience these feelings, but remain focused on the task at hand.

When you meet your new pet, approach them with patience and gentleness. Remember that this is a significant change for them as well, and they may be feeling a range of emotions, from curiosity to apprehension. Speak softly and move slowly, allowing the pet to become familiar with your presence. This initial interaction sets the tone for your relationship and helps build trust.

Before leaving the adoption center, take the time to ask any remaining questions you may have about your pet's history, health, and care requirements. The staff at the shelter are valuable resources, equipped with knowledge and experience to guide you in providing the best possible care for your new companion. Inquire about feeding schedules, exercise needs, and any medical conditions or treatments your pet may require.

Once you've completed the adoption process, it's time to embark on the journey home. Ensure that your pet is safely secured in a carrier or with a leash, and take care to drive calmly and steadily. The journey home can be a stressful experience for a pet, especially if they are unfamiliar with car travel. Speaking reassuringly and maintaining a tranquil environment can help ease their anxiety.

Upon arriving home, introduce your pet to their new surroundings gradually. Begin by allowing them to explore a designated area, such as a single room, before expanding their access to the rest of the house. This approach helps prevent overwhelming your pet and allows them to acclimate at their own pace. Provide them with a comfortable space to rest, complete with bedding, food, and water.

Establishing a routine is crucial in helping your pet adjust to their new environment. Consistency in feeding times, walks, and play sessions provides a sense of security and predictability. Over time, your pet will come to understand and anticipate these routines, fostering a sense of belonging and stability.

As you settle into life with your new pet, be prepared for an adjustment period. It's normal for both you and your pet to experience a learning curve as you navigate this new relationship. Be patient and understanding, recognizing that building trust and familiarity takes time. Celebrate small victories and milestones, such as your pet's first successful walk or their comfort in exploring new areas of the home.

Socialization is an important aspect of your pet's development and well-being. Gradually introduce them to new people, environments, and experiences, ensuring that these interactions are positive and rewarding. This exposure helps your pet build confidence and adaptability, essential traits for a harmonious life together.

Training is another key component of your pet's integration into your home. Whether you're teaching basic commands or addressing specific behavioral issues, consistency and positive reinforcement are essential. Approach training with patience and encouragement, celebrating your pet's progress and understanding that setbacks are a natural part of the learning process.

Throughout this journey, it's important to prioritize your pet's health and well-being. Schedule a visit to the veterinarian for a comprehensive check-up and to establish a vaccination and preventative care plan. Regular veterinary visits are crucial in maintaining your pet's health and addressing any concerns that may arise.

Adoption day is a transformative experience, marking the beginning of a lifelong bond between you and your pet. By approaching this day with preparation, patience, and an open heart, you set the stage for a fulfilling and rewarding relationship. Embrace the joys and challenges of pet ownership, knowing that the love and companionship you share will enrich your life in countless ways.

Chapter 3: Bringing Your New Friend Home

Preparing Your Home Environment

Creating a welcoming and safe environment for your new pet is an essential step in ensuring their successful integration into your home. The process of preparing your home involves thoughtful planning and attention to detail, as it sets the foundation for a harmonious relationship between you and your new companion. By considering the specific needs of your pet, you can create a space that promotes their well-being and fosters a sense of security.

Begin by assessing the layout of your home and identifying areas that may require modification to accommodate your pet. Consider the size and breed of your pet, as these factors will influence the amount of space they need and the type of environment that will best suit them. For instance, larger dogs may require more room to move around, while smaller pets may feel more comfortable in a cozier setting. Take note of any potential hazards, such as sharp edges, toxic plants, or small objects that could be swallowed, and take steps to mitigate these risks.

Designate a specific area in your home where your pet can feel safe and comfortable. This space should be equipped with all the essentials, including a bed, food and water dishes, and toys. Providing a dedicated area helps your pet establish a sense of territory and belonging, which is crucial for their emotional well-being. Ensure that this space is easily accessible and free from excessive noise or disturbances, allowing your pet to retreat and relax when needed.

Consider the flooring in your home, as it can impact your pet's comfort and safety. Hardwood or tile floors may be slippery for some pets, particularly older animals or those with mobility issues. Placing rugs or mats in key areas can provide traction and prevent accidents. Additionally, be mindful of any areas where your pet may be prone to slipping or falling, such as stairs or elevated surfaces, and take precautions to prevent injuries.

Pet-proofing your home is a vital aspect of preparation. This involves securing any items that could pose a danger to your pet, such as cleaning supplies, medications, or electrical cords. Store these items out of reach or in locked cabinets to prevent accidental ingestion or injury. Additionally, ensure that windows and doors are securely closed to prevent your pet from escaping or becoming lost.

If you have other pets in the home, it's important to consider their needs and how they will interact with the new addition. Gradual introductions and supervised interactions can help ease the transition and prevent conflicts. Monitor their behavior closely and be prepared to intervene if necessary, ensuring that all pets feel safe and respected in their shared environment.

Establishing a routine is key to helping your pet adjust to their new home. Consistent feeding times, walks, and play sessions provide structure and predictability, which can be comforting for your pet. Over time, they will come to understand and anticipate these routines, fostering a sense of stability and security.

Incorporating enrichment activities into your pet's daily routine can enhance their quality of life and prevent boredom. This may include interactive toys, puzzle feeders, or training exercises that engage their mind and body. Providing opportunities for mental and physical stimulation is essential for your pet's overall well-being and can help prevent behavioral issues.

Consider the climate and temperature of your home, as these factors can impact your pet's comfort. Ensure that your home is adequately heated or cooled, depending on the season, and provide additional bedding or blankets if needed. Be mindful of any drafts or areas where your pet may be exposed to extreme temperatures, and take steps to create a comfortable environment.

Regular cleaning and maintenance of your pet's living area are crucial for their health and hygiene. This includes washing bedding, cleaning food and water dishes, and removing any waste or debris. Maintaining a clean environment helps prevent the spread of disease and ensures that your pet remains healthy and happy.

Finally, take the time to educate yourself about your pet's specific needs and preferences. Understanding their behavior, dietary requirements, and health considerations will enable you to provide the best possible care. This knowledge will also help you anticipate any challenges that may arise and equip you with the tools to address them effectively.

Preparing your home environment is a thoughtful and deliberate process that lays the groundwork for a successful and fulfilling relationship with your new pet. By considering their unique needs and creating a safe and nurturing space, you set the stage for a lifetime of companionship and joy. Embrace the journey of pet ownership with an open heart and a commitment to providing the love and care your pet deserves.

Essential Supplies and Equipment

Equipping yourself with the right supplies and equipment is a crucial step in ensuring the well-being and happiness of your new pet. The process of gathering these essentials involves careful consideration of your pet's specific needs, as well as an understanding of the various products available on the market. By investing in quality items, you can create a comfortable and nurturing environment that supports your pet's health and development.

Begin by considering the basic necessities that every pet requires, such as food and water dishes. These should be sturdy, easy to clean, and appropriately sized for your pet. Stainless steel or ceramic bowls are often recommended due to their durability and resistance to bacteria. Ensure that the dishes are placed in a quiet, accessible area where your pet can eat and drink without disturbance.

Selecting the right food for your pet is another critical aspect of preparation. Consult with your veterinarian to determine the best diet for your pet's age, breed, and health status. Whether you choose commercial pet food or a homemade diet, it's important to provide balanced nutrition that meets your pet's dietary needs. Be mindful of portion sizes and feeding schedules, as overfeeding can lead to obesity and other health issues.

A comfortable bed is essential for your pet's rest and relaxation. Choose a bed that is appropriately sized and provides adequate support for your pet's body. Orthopedic beds are particularly beneficial for older pets or those with joint issues, as they offer additional cushioning and support. Place the bed in a quiet, draft-free area where your pet can sleep undisturbed.

Toys and enrichment activities play a vital role in your pet's mental and physical well-being. Interactive toys, such as puzzle feeders or treat-dispensing balls, can provide mental stimulation and prevent boredom. Chew toys are also important for dental health, particularly for dogs, as they help clean teeth and massage gums. Rotate toys regularly to keep your pet engaged and interested.

Grooming supplies are another essential component of pet care. Depending on your pet's breed and coat type, you may need brushes, combs, nail clippers, and shampoo. Regular grooming helps maintain your pet's coat and skin health, reduces shedding, and strengthens the bond between you and your pet. Establish a grooming routine that suits your pet's needs and be gentle and patient during the process.

For pets that require regular exercise, such as dogs, a sturdy leash and collar or harness are necessary. Choose a leash that is comfortable to hold and provides adequate control, and ensure that the collar or harness fits properly without causing discomfort. Reflective or LED accessories can enhance visibility during nighttime walks, ensuring the safety of both you and your pet.

A secure crate or carrier is essential for travel and transportation. Select a crate that is appropriately sized for your pet, allowing them to stand, turn around, and lie down comfortably. Crates can also serve as a safe space for your pet at home, providing a sense of security and comfort. Introduce the crate gradually and use positive reinforcement to encourage your pet to enter willingly.

For pets with specific health needs, additional supplies may be required. This could include medications, supplements, or specialized equipment, such as ramps or mobility aids. Consult with your veterinarian to determine the best course of action and ensure that you have the necessary supplies on hand.

Pet identification is crucial for your pet's safety and security. A collar with an ID tag containing your contact information is a simple yet effective way to ensure your pet can be returned to you if they become lost. Microchipping is another option that provides a permanent form of identification, increasing the likelihood of a safe return.

Cleaning supplies are an often-overlooked aspect of pet ownership, yet they are essential for maintaining a hygienic environment. Stock up on pet-safe cleaning products, such as enzymatic cleaners for accidents and lint rollers for fur removal. Regular cleaning helps prevent the spread of bacteria and allergens, ensuring a healthy home for both you and your pet.

Finally, consider the specific needs of your pet's species or breed. For example, reptiles may require heat lamps and specialized enclosures, while birds may need perches and toys for mental stimulation. Research your pet's unique requirements and invest in the necessary equipment to provide a comfortable and enriching environment.

By gathering the essential supplies and equipment, you lay the foundation for a successful and fulfilling relationship with your pet. Thoughtful preparation and attention to detail ensure that your pet's needs are met, allowing them to thrive in their new home. Embrace the journey of pet ownership with confidence, knowing that you are equipped to provide the love and care your pet deserves.

Introducing Your Pet to Family Members

Bringing a new pet into your home is an exciting and transformative experience, not just for you but for your entire family. The introduction process is a delicate dance that requires patience, understanding, and a touch of strategy to ensure a harmonious integration. Each family member, whether human or animal, will have their own reactions and adjustments to make. By approaching this transition with care, you can foster a loving and supportive environment for your new pet.

Begin by preparing your family for the arrival of the new pet. Discuss the responsibilities and changes that will come with this addition, ensuring that everyone understands their role in the pet's care. Assign specific tasks, such as feeding, walking, or grooming, to different family members based on their abilities and interests. This not only distributes the workload but also helps each person form a bond with the pet.

When introducing your pet to the family, it's important to create a calm and welcoming atmosphere. Choose a quiet time when the household is relaxed, avoiding moments of high activity or stress. Allow the pet to explore their new surroundings at their own pace, providing them with a safe space where they can retreat if they feel overwhelmed. This could be a designated room or a cozy corner with their bed and toys.

For families with children, it's crucial to teach them how to interact with the new pet appropriately. Explain the importance of gentle handling and respecting the pet's boundaries. Encourage children to approach the pet slowly and quietly, allowing the animal to sniff and become familiar with them. Supervise all interactions initially to ensure that both the pet and the children are comfortable and safe.

Existing pets in the household require special consideration during this transition. The introduction should be gradual and controlled, allowing both the new and existing pets to acclimate to each other's presence. Start by exchanging scents, such as swapping bedding or toys, to familiarize them with each other's smell. When it's time for a face-to-face meeting, choose a neutral space where neither pet feels territorial. Keep the initial interactions short and positive, rewarding both pets with treats and praise for calm behavior.

Monitor the dynamics between the new pet and existing pets closely. Look for signs of stress or aggression, such as growling, hissing, or avoidance, and intervene if necessary. It's important to remain patient and give the animals time to adjust to each other's presence. In some cases, it may take weeks or even months for pets to fully accept one another, so persistence and consistency are key.

Communication is vital during this period of adjustment. Encourage family members to express their feelings and concerns about the new pet, fostering an open dialogue that allows everyone to feel heard and supported. Address any issues or challenges that arise promptly, working together to find solutions that benefit both the pet and the family.

As the new pet becomes more comfortable in their environment, gradually introduce them to different areas of the home and various family activities. This helps them become accustomed to the household routine and strengthens their bond with each family member. Include the pet in family gatherings, walks, or playtime, ensuring they feel like a valued part of the family unit.

Training and socialization are essential components of a successful introduction. Establish a consistent routine for feeding, exercise, and training, providing the pet with structure and predictability. Positive reinforcement techniques, such as treats and praise, can be highly effective in encouraging desired behaviors and building trust between the pet and family members.

For pets with specific behavioral needs, consider seeking the guidance of a professional trainer or behaviorist. They can provide valuable insights and strategies for addressing challenges and ensuring a smooth integration into the family. This support can be particularly beneficial for families with limited experience in pet ownership or those facing complex behavioral issues.

Celebrate the milestones and successes along the way, acknowledging the progress made by both the pet and the family. Whether it's the first time the pet responds to a command or a peaceful interaction between pets, these moments are a testament to the effort and dedication invested in the process.

Ultimately, the introduction of a new pet to your family is a journey of growth and discovery. It requires patience, empathy, and a willingness to adapt to the needs of both the pet and the family. By approaching this transition with care and consideration, you can create a nurturing environment where your pet feels loved and secure, and your family enjoys the companionship and joy that a new pet brings.

The First 24 Hours: Settling In

The first 24 hours with a new pet are a whirlwind of emotions and experiences, both for you and your new companion. This initial period sets the tone for your pet's transition into their new home, and it's crucial to approach it with a blend of preparation, patience, and empathy. As you embark on this journey, consider the world from your pet's perspective: everything is new, unfamiliar, and potentially overwhelming. Your role is to provide a sense of security and comfort as they navigate this fresh chapter of their life.

Before your pet arrives, ensure that your home is ready to welcome them. Create a designated space where they can retreat and feel safe. This area should include a comfortable bed, fresh water, and some toys to keep them entertained. If you have a cat, a litter box should be placed in a quiet, accessible location. For dogs, consider setting up a crate or a gated area where they can relax without feeling confined. This space will serve as their sanctuary, a place they can call their own as they acclimate to their new surroundings.

Once your pet arrives, give them time to explore their new environment at their own pace. Resist the urge to overwhelm them with attention or introduce them to every room in the house immediately. Instead, allow them to investigate their designated area first, gradually expanding their exploration as they become more comfortable. Keep in mind that each pet is unique; some may be eager to explore, while others may be more reserved and cautious.

During these first hours, it's important to establish a routine that will provide your pet with a sense of stability and predictability. Begin by setting regular feeding times, ensuring that your pet knows when to expect their meals. This not only helps with their adjustment but also aids in establishing a bond between you and your pet. Use mealtime as an opportunity to interact positively, offering gentle words and affection as they eat.

As your pet settles in, pay close attention to their body language and behavior. Look for signs of stress or anxiety, such as pacing, excessive panting, or hiding. If your pet seems overwhelmed, give them space and time to adjust. Speak to them in a calm, soothing voice, and offer treats or toys to help them associate their new environment with positive experiences. Remember, patience is key; your pet is learning to trust you and their new surroundings.

Introduce your pet to family members gradually, ensuring that each interaction is calm and positive. Encourage family members to approach the pet slowly and allow the animal to initiate contact. This helps build trust and prevents your pet from feeling threatened or overwhelmed. For families with children, it's essential to teach them how to interact with the pet gently and respectfully, emphasizing the importance of boundaries and personal space.

During this initial period, it's also important to establish boundaries and house rules. If there are areas of the home that are off-limits to your pet, make this clear from the start. Use baby gates or closed doors to restrict access, and provide plenty of positive reinforcement when your pet respects these boundaries. Consistency is crucial in helping your pet understand what is expected of them.

Socialization is another key aspect of the first 24 hours. While it's important not to overwhelm your pet with too many new experiences at once, gentle exposure to different sights, sounds, and smells can help them acclimate to their new environment. Take your dog for a short walk around the neighborhood, allowing them to sniff and explore at their own pace. For cats, consider placing a perch near a window where they can observe the outside world from a safe distance.

As the day progresses, spend quality time with your pet, engaging in activities that foster bonding and trust. This could include playing with toys, gentle grooming, or simply sitting together in a quiet space. These interactions help your pet associate you with positive experiences and reinforce the bond between you.

As night falls, ensure that your pet has a comfortable and secure place to sleep. For dogs, this might mean a cozy bed in their crate or a designated spot in your bedroom. Cats may prefer a soft blanket in a quiet corner or a perch where they can observe their surroundings. Providing a consistent sleeping area helps your pet feel secure and establishes a routine that will aid in their adjustment.

Throughout these first 24 hours, remain attentive to your pet's needs and emotions. Be patient and understanding, recognizing that this is a significant transition for them. Celebrate small victories, such as your pet eating their first meal or exploring a new part of the house, as these moments are milestones in their journey to becoming a part of your family.

In the end, the first day with your new pet is just the beginning of a lifelong relationship filled with love, companionship, and shared experiences. By approaching this initial period with care and empathy, you lay the foundation for a strong bond and a harmonious life together. Your pet will come to see you as their source of comfort and security, and you will gain a loyal and loving companion who enriches your life in countless ways.

Establishing a Routine

Establishing a routine is a cornerstone of creating a harmonious and balanced life for both you and your pet. A well-structured routine provides predictability and security, which are essential for your pet's well-being. It also helps you manage your time effectively, ensuring that your pet's needs are met consistently. The process of establishing a routine involves understanding your pet's natural rhythms and aligning them with your daily schedule, creating a seamless integration of your lives.

Begin by observing your pet's behavior and energy levels throughout the day. Take note of when they seem most active, when they prefer to rest, and when they exhibit signs of hunger or the need for a bathroom break. This information will serve as the foundation for crafting a routine that respects their natural inclinations while accommodating your lifestyle. For instance, if your dog is particularly energetic in the morning, this might be the ideal time for a brisk walk or play session. Conversely, if your cat is more active in the evening, consider scheduling interactive playtime during those hours.

Feeding is a critical component of any pet's routine. Establish regular meal times that align with your pet's natural hunger cues. Consistency in feeding not only aids in digestion but also reinforces a sense of security. For dogs, two meals a day—one in the morning and one in the evening—are typically sufficient. Cats, on the other hand, may prefer smaller, more frequent meals. Regardless of the specifics, ensure that fresh water is always available.

Exercise is another vital aspect of a pet's routine. Regular physical activity promotes physical health, mental stimulation, and emotional well-being. For dogs, daily walks are essential, providing not only exercise but also opportunities for socialization and exploration. The length and intensity of the walk should be tailored to your dog's breed, age, and energy level. In addition to walks, consider incorporating play sessions that engage your dog's natural instincts, such as fetch or tug-of-war.

Cats, while often perceived as more independent, also benefit from regular exercise. Interactive toys, such as feather wands or laser pointers, can provide mental and physical stimulation. Additionally, consider setting up a cat tree or perch near a window, allowing your cat to observe the outside world and engage in natural behaviors like climbing and scratching.

Training and mental stimulation are crucial components of a well-rounded routine. For dogs, daily training sessions reinforce obedience and strengthen the bond between you and your pet. These sessions need not be lengthy; even a few minutes a day can yield significant results. Focus on basic commands, such as sit, stay, and come, gradually introducing more complex tasks as your dog progresses. Positive reinforcement, in the form of treats or praise, is key to successful training.

Cats, too, can benefit from mental stimulation. Puzzle feeders and treat-dispensing toys encourage problem-solving and provide enrichment. Additionally, consider teaching your cat simple tricks, such as high-five or sit, using clicker training techniques. These activities not only engage your cat's mind but also enhance your relationship.

Rest and relaxation are equally important in a pet's routine. Ensure that your pet has a comfortable and quiet place to rest, free from disturbances. Dogs may appreciate a cozy bed in a quiet corner, while cats often seek out elevated perches or secluded nooks. Respect your pet's need for downtime, and avoid interrupting their rest unless necessary.

Socialization is another key element of a balanced routine. For dogs, regular interactions with other dogs and people are essential for developing social skills and preventing behavioral issues. Arrange playdates with other dogs or visit a local dog park, ensuring that these interactions are positive and supervised. Cats, while generally more solitary, can also benefit from socialization. Introduce them to new people gradually, allowing them to approach at their own pace.

Grooming is an often-overlooked aspect of a pet's routine, yet it plays a crucial role in maintaining their health and well-being.

Regular brushing helps reduce shedding and prevents matting, while also providing an opportunity to check for any skin issues or parasites. For dogs, regular nail trims and dental care are essential. Cats, particularly those with long hair, may require more frequent grooming to prevent tangles and hairballs.

As you establish a routine, remain flexible and open to adjustments. Life is unpredictable, and there will be days when your schedule deviates from the norm. The key is to maintain consistency as much as possible while adapting to changes as needed. Your pet will appreciate the stability that a routine provides, even if it occasionally requires modification.

Communication is vital in maintaining a successful routine. Pay attention to your pet's cues and signals, and be responsive to their needs. If your pet seems restless or anxious, consider whether their routine requires adjustment. Perhaps they need more exercise, mental stimulation, or simply more quality time with you. By remaining attuned to your pet's needs, you can ensure that their routine continues to support their overall well-being.

Incorporating a routine into your daily life not only benefits your pet but also enhances your own sense of structure and purpose. The predictability of a routine can reduce stress and create a more harmonious household. As you and your pet settle into this rhythm, you'll find that the bonds of trust and companionship grow stronger, enriching your lives in countless ways.

Chapter 4: Building a Strong Relationship

Bonding Techniques for New Pets

Bringing a new pet into your home is an exciting and transformative experience, yet it also requires patience and understanding to build a strong bond. The initial days and weeks are crucial for establishing trust and creating a foundation for a lifelong relationship. Bonding with a new pet involves a combination of time, attention, and empathy, as well as an understanding of your pet's unique personality and needs.

The first step in bonding with your new pet is to create a welcoming and safe environment. This means preparing your home to accommodate their needs, ensuring they have a designated space where they can feel secure. For a dog, this might be a cozy bed in a quiet corner, while a cat may prefer a secluded nook or a perch by a window. Providing familiar items, such as a blanket or toy from their previous environment, can also help ease the transition.

Once your pet is settled, it's important to establish a routine that incorporates regular interaction and engagement. Consistency is key, as it helps your pet understand what to expect and builds a sense of security. Spend time each day engaging in activities that your pet enjoys, whether it's playing fetch with a dog or using interactive toys with a cat. These shared experiences not only provide physical and mental stimulation but also strengthen the bond between you and your pet.

Communication plays a vital role in bonding. Pay attention to your pet's body language and vocalizations, as these are their primary means of expressing themselves. Dogs, for example, may wag their tails or bark to convey excitement, while cats might purr or meow to communicate contentment or a desire for attention. By learning to interpret these signals, you can respond appropriately and build trust with your pet.

Positive reinforcement is another effective bonding technique. Rewarding your pet with treats, praise, or affection when they exhibit desired behaviors encourages them to repeat those actions. This approach is particularly useful during training sessions, as it reinforces the connection between you and your pet. For dogs, basic obedience training can be a rewarding experience that enhances communication and mutual respect. Cats, while often more independent, can also benefit from positive reinforcement when learning new tricks or using a scratching post.

Spending quality time together is essential for building a strong bond. This doesn't always mean engaging in structured activities; sometimes, simply being present with your pet can be enough. Sit quietly with your pet, allowing them to approach you on their terms. This can be especially important for shy or anxious animals, as it demonstrates patience and understanding. Over time, your pet will come to associate your presence with comfort and security.

Socialization is another important aspect of bonding, particularly for dogs. Exposing your pet to a variety of people, animals, and environments helps them develop confidence and adaptability. Arrange playdates with other dogs or visit a local dog park, ensuring that these interactions are positive and supervised. For cats, socialization may involve introducing them to new people gradually, allowing them to explore their surroundings at their own pace.

Grooming is a bonding activity that is often overlooked. Regular grooming sessions not only help maintain your pet's physical health but also provide an opportunity for close contact and interaction. Brushing your dog's coat or gently stroking your cat can be a calming and enjoyable experience for both of you. Additionally, grooming allows you to check for any health issues, such as skin irritations or parasites, further demonstrating your care and attention.

Patience is crucial when bonding with a new pet. Every animal is unique, and some may take longer to adjust to their new environment than others. It's important to respect your pet's boundaries and allow them to set the pace for interaction. Forcing a pet to engage before they're ready can lead to stress and anxiety, hindering the bonding process. Instead, focus on creating positive experiences and gradually building trust over time.

Understanding your pet's background can also aid in the bonding process. If your pet has come from a shelter or rescue, they may have experienced trauma or neglect in the past. Being aware of their history can help you approach them with empathy and compassion, tailoring your interactions to meet their specific needs. For instance, a dog that has been mistreated may require extra patience and gentle handling, while a cat that has been rehomed multiple times may need reassurance and stability.

Incorporating play into your daily routine is an effective way to bond with your pet. Playtime provides an outlet for energy and encourages natural behaviors, such as chasing, pouncing, or retrieving. For dogs, games like fetch or tug-of-war can be both physically and mentally stimulating. Cats, on the other hand, may enjoy chasing a feather wand or batting at a toy mouse. These activities not only strengthen your bond but also contribute to your pet's overall well-being.

As you bond with your new pet, it's important to remain flexible and open to change. Your pet's needs and preferences may evolve over time, and being attuned to these changes will help you maintain a strong connection. Regularly assess your pet's behavior and adjust your interactions accordingly, ensuring that your bond continues to grow and flourish.

Building a bond with a new pet is a journey that requires time, effort, and understanding. By creating a safe and welcoming environment, establishing a routine, and engaging in positive interactions, you can foster a deep and lasting connection with your pet. This bond will not only enhance your pet's quality of life but also bring joy and fulfillment to your own.

Understanding Body Language and Signals

Understanding the body language and signals of your pet is akin to learning a new language, one that is rich with nuance and emotion. This silent communication is the key to unlocking a deeper connection with your furry companion, allowing you to respond to their needs and emotions with empathy and precision. Each species, and indeed each individual animal, has its own unique set of signals that convey a wide range of feelings and intentions.

Dogs, for instance, are expressive creatures whose body language can reveal much about their emotional state. A wagging tail is often interpreted as a sign of happiness, but the context and position of the tail can alter its meaning. A high, stiff wag might indicate excitement or alertness, while a low, slow wag could suggest insecurity or submission. Similarly, a dog's ears and eyes are telling indicators. Ears perked forward can signal curiosity or interest, whereas ears pinned back might denote fear or anxiety. A soft gaze often reflects contentment, while a hard stare can be a warning sign of aggression or discomfort.

Cats, on the other hand, are more subtle in their expressions. Their tails, too, are communicative tools. A tail held high typically signifies confidence and friendliness, while a puffed-up tail is a clear sign of fear or agitation. The position of a cat's ears can also provide insight into their mood. Forward-facing ears suggest curiosity or playfulness, while flattened ears may indicate irritation or fear. A cat's eyes are equally expressive; slow blinking is a sign of trust and affection, whereas dilated pupils can signal excitement or fear.

Beyond these general signals, it's important to recognize that each pet has its own personality and quirks. Observing your pet's behavior in various situations will help you understand their unique communication style. For example, some dogs may bark to express excitement, while others might do so out of anxiety. Similarly, a cat may purr when content, but some cats also purr when they're in pain or stressed. By paying close attention to your pet's individual signals, you can better interpret their needs and emotions.

Understanding body language is not just about recognizing signs of happiness or distress; it's also about identifying subtle cues that can prevent misunderstandings or conflicts. For instance, a dog that yawns or licks its lips may be trying to calm itself in a stressful situation. These are known as "calming signals," and they can be crucial in de-escalating potential conflicts with other animals or humans. Similarly, a cat that flicks its tail or flattens its ears may be signaling that it needs space or is feeling threatened.

In addition to observing your pet's body language, it's important to consider the context in which these signals occur. A dog that growls while playing tug-of-war may not be aggressive, but rather engaged in a spirited game. Conversely, a cat that hisses when approached may be feeling cornered or threatened. By taking into account the environment and circumstances, you can more accurately interpret your pet's signals and respond appropriately.

Building a strong bond with your pet involves not only understanding their body language but also using your own body language to communicate effectively. Animals are highly perceptive and can pick up on subtle cues from their human companions. Maintaining a relaxed posture and using gentle, deliberate movements can help convey calmness and reassurance. Similarly, using a soft, soothing voice can reinforce positive interactions and build trust.

Training sessions provide an excellent opportunity to practice interpreting and responding to your pet's body language. Positive reinforcement techniques, such as rewarding desired behaviors with treats or praise, can strengthen the bond between you and your pet while enhancing communication. During training, pay attention to your pet's signals to ensure they are comfortable and engaged. If your pet shows signs of stress or frustration, such as yawning, panting, or avoiding eye contact, it may be time to take a break or adjust your approach.

Socialization is another important aspect of understanding body language and signals. Exposing your pet to a variety of people, animals, and environments can help them develop confidence and adaptability. During these interactions, observe how your pet communicates with others and use this information to guide your responses. For example, if your dog shows signs of fear or aggression when meeting new dogs, you can work on gradually desensitizing them to these situations in a controlled and positive manner.

Patience and consistency are key when learning to interpret your pet's body language. It takes time to become fluent in this silent language, and mistakes are a natural part of the learning process. By remaining observant and open-minded, you can deepen your understanding of your pet's signals and strengthen your relationship.

Understanding body language and signals is an ongoing journey that evolves as you and your pet grow together. As you become more attuned to your pet's unique communication style, you'll find that your bond becomes richer and more rewarding. This mutual understanding not only enhances your pet's quality of life but also brings joy and fulfillment to your own.

Positive Reinforcement and Training

Training a pet is a journey that requires patience, understanding, and a touch of creativity. Positive reinforcement stands as one of the most effective and humane methods to guide your pet's behavior. This approach focuses on rewarding desired behaviors, thereby encouraging their repetition. Unlike punitive measures, which can instill fear and anxiety, positive reinforcement fosters a trusting and joyful relationship between you and your pet.

Imagine a scenario where a dog named Max is learning to sit on command. Each time Max successfully sits, he receives a treat and a gentle pat on the head. Over time, Max associates the act of sitting with positive outcomes, making him more likely to repeat the behavior. This simple yet powerful concept lies at the heart of positive reinforcement.

The first step in implementing this training method is identifying what motivates your pet. For many animals, food is a powerful incentive. Small, tasty treats can be used as rewards, but it's important to ensure they are healthy and appropriate for your pet's diet. Some pets may respond better to verbal praise, affection, or playtime. Observing your pet's preferences will help you tailor the rewards to their liking, making the training process more effective.

Consistency is crucial when using positive reinforcement. Each time your pet exhibits the desired behavior, they should receive a reward. This consistency helps reinforce the connection between the behavior and the positive outcome. It's also important to deliver the reward immediately after the behavior occurs, so your pet can clearly associate the two.

Timing plays a significant role in the success of positive reinforcement. If the reward is given too late, your pet may not understand which behavior is being reinforced. For instance, if Max sits but receives his treat after he stands up again, he might not make the connection between sitting and the reward. Being prompt with rewards ensures clarity and strengthens the learning process.

As your pet becomes more proficient in a particular behavior, you can gradually reduce the frequency of rewards. This process, known as "fading," helps your pet transition from expecting a treat every time to performing the behavior with less frequent reinforcement. Eventually, verbal praise or affection can replace treats as the primary reward, maintaining the behavior without over-reliance on food incentives.

Incorporating positive reinforcement into daily routines can enhance its effectiveness. For example, if you're teaching your dog to come when called, practice this command during walks or playtime. When your dog responds correctly, reward them with a treat or a game of fetch. This integration into everyday activities helps reinforce the behavior in various contexts, making it more reliable.

Training sessions should be kept short and engaging to maintain your pet's interest. Animals, like humans, can become bored or frustrated if sessions are too long or repetitive. Aim for multiple short sessions throughout the day, each lasting no more than 10 to 15 minutes. This approach keeps your pet motivated and eager to learn.

Positive reinforcement is not limited to teaching basic commands; it can also be used to address behavioral issues. For instance, if your cat scratches furniture, you can redirect this behavior by providing a scratching post and rewarding your cat each time they use it. Over time, your cat will learn that using the scratching post results in positive outcomes, reducing the likelihood of unwanted scratching.

Socialization is another area where positive reinforcement can be invaluable. Introducing your pet to new people, animals, and environments can be a daunting task, but rewarding calm and friendly behavior can ease the process. If your dog remains relaxed when meeting a new person, offer a treat or praise to reinforce this positive interaction. Gradually, your pet will become more comfortable and confident in social situations.

While positive reinforcement is a powerful tool, it's important to remain patient and understanding throughout the training process. Every pet learns at their own pace, and setbacks are a natural part of the journey. If your pet struggles with a particular behavior, consider breaking it down into smaller, more manageable steps. For example, if you're teaching your dog to roll over, start by rewarding them for lying down, then gradually build up to the full behavior.

Avoiding punishment is a key principle of positive reinforcement. Punitive measures can damage the bond between you and your pet, leading to fear and mistrust. Instead, focus on redirecting unwanted behaviors and reinforcing positive ones. If your pet makes a mistake, simply withhold the reward and try again. This approach encourages learning without instilling fear or anxiety.

Communication is an essential component of successful training. Using clear, consistent cues helps your pet understand what is expected of them. Choose simple commands and use them consistently across all training sessions. For example, if you're teaching your dog to sit, use the word "sit" each time, rather than alternating between "sit" and "down." This consistency helps your pet associate the command with the desired behavior.

Involving the whole family in the training process can also enhance its effectiveness. Ensure that everyone uses the same commands and rewards to maintain consistency. This unified approach prevents confusion and reinforces the learning process.

Positive reinforcement is a versatile and compassionate training method that can be adapted to suit the needs of any pet. By focusing on rewarding desired behaviors, you create an environment where your pet feels safe, valued, and motivated to learn. This approach not only strengthens the bond between you and your pet but also lays the foundation for a lifetime of positive interactions and shared experiences.

Socialization Strategies

Socialization is a crucial aspect of raising a well-adjusted pet, and it begins the moment your furry companion enters your life. The process involves exposing your pet to a variety of experiences, environments, people, and other animals to help them develop confidence and adaptability. A well-socialized pet is more likely to be friendly, calm, and less prone to anxiety or aggression in unfamiliar situations. The key to successful socialization lies in a thoughtful and gradual approach, ensuring that each new experience is positive and enriching.

Consider the story of Bella, a young Labrador Retriever who was introduced to her new home at eight weeks old. Her owner, Sarah, understood the importance of socialization and embarked on a journey to expose Bella to the world around her. Sarah began by introducing Bella to different rooms in the house, allowing her to explore at her own pace. She provided plenty of praise and treats to reinforce Bella's curiosity and bravery.

Once Bella was comfortable in her home environment, Sarah expanded her socialization efforts to include the outdoors. Short walks around the neighborhood introduced Bella to various sights, sounds, and smells. During these walks, Bella encountered other dogs, children playing, and the occasional passing car. Each interaction was met with encouragement and rewards, helping Bella associate these new experiences with positive outcomes.

Introducing your pet to a diverse range of people is another essential component of socialization. Pets that are accustomed to different types of people—such as those with varying ages, appearances, and voices—are less likely to react fearfully or aggressively in social situations. Sarah invited friends and family members to visit, ensuring that each interaction was calm and positive. Bella was allowed to approach new people at her own pace, receiving treats and gentle petting as a reward for her friendly behavior.

Socialization also involves familiarizing your pet with other animals. For dogs, this can mean meeting other dogs in controlled settings, such as a dog park or a friend's backyard. It's important to monitor these interactions closely, ensuring that they remain positive and stress-free. If Bella showed signs of discomfort or fear, Sarah would calmly remove her from the situation and try again later, gradually building Bella's confidence around other dogs.

Cats, too, benefit from socialization, though their process may differ slightly from that of dogs. Introducing a cat to new environments and people should be done gradually, allowing the cat to explore at their own pace. Providing hiding spots and high perches can help a cat feel secure while they acclimate to new surroundings. Positive reinforcement, such as treats or playtime, can encourage a cat to engage with their environment and the people within it.

Exposure to different environments is another critical aspect of socialization. Taking your pet on car rides, visiting pet-friendly stores, or exploring new parks can help them become accustomed to a variety of settings. Each new environment presents unique stimuli, and by gradually introducing your pet to these experiences, you help them develop resilience and adaptability.

It's important to remember that socialization is not a one-time event but an ongoing process. Regular exposure to new experiences helps reinforce your pet's social skills and prevents regression. As Bella grew older, Sarah continued to introduce her to new environments and experiences, ensuring that Bella remained confident and well-adjusted.

While socialization is essential, it's equally important to recognize your pet's limits. Pushing a pet too quickly or exposing them to overwhelming situations can lead to fear and anxiety. Pay close attention to your pet's body language and behavior, and be prepared to adjust your approach if necessary. Signs of stress, such as cowering, growling, or excessive panting, indicate that your pet may need a break or a slower introduction to the new experience.

For pets that have missed early socialization opportunities, such as rescue animals or those adopted later in life, the process may require additional patience and care. Gradual exposure and positive reinforcement remain key components, but it's important to be mindful of any past traumas or fears that may affect your pet's behavior. Working with a professional trainer or behaviorist can provide valuable guidance and support in these situations.

Socialization is a rewarding journey that strengthens the bond between you and your pet. By providing your pet with a wide range of positive experiences, you help them develop the confidence and social skills needed to navigate the world with ease. This foundation not only enhances your pet's quality of life but also fosters a harmonious relationship built on trust and understanding.

Creating a Safe and Loving Environment

Creating a safe and loving environment for your pet is foundational to their well-being and happiness. This chapter delves into the essential elements that contribute to a nurturing home, ensuring your pet feels secure, cherished, and part of the family. The journey begins with understanding the unique needs of your pet, whether they are a dog, cat, bird, or any other companion animal. Each species has its own requirements for space, comfort, and interaction, and recognizing these needs is the first step in crafting a harmonious living space.

Consider the story of Max, a rescued tabby cat who found his forever home with Emily. Max had spent his early life in a shelter, and Emily was determined to provide him with a sanctuary where he could thrive. She began by designating a quiet room as Max's personal space, complete with a cozy bed, litter box, and an array of toys. This room served as a safe haven where Max could retreat whenever he felt overwhelmed or needed solitude.

Safety is paramount in any pet-friendly environment. For dogs and cats, this means securing potential hazards such as electrical cords, toxic plants, and small objects that could be swallowed. Installing baby gates or pet barriers can prevent access to areas that may pose a risk, such as staircases or kitchens. Emily ensured that Max's environment was free from dangers by conducting a thorough inspection of her home, removing any items that could harm her curious feline friend.

Creating a loving environment extends beyond physical safety; it encompasses emotional security as well. Pets thrive on routine and predictability, which help them feel grounded and secure. Establishing a consistent schedule for feeding, playtime, and rest can provide your pet with a sense of stability. Emily found that Max responded positively to a regular routine, eagerly anticipating mealtimes and play sessions, which strengthened their bond.

Interaction and companionship are vital components of a loving environment. Pets are social creatures, and they flourish when they feel connected to their human family. Spending quality time with your pet through play, training, or simply relaxing together fosters a deep sense of belonging. Emily made it a point to engage with Max daily, whether through interactive play with feather toys or quiet moments of petting and affection. These interactions not only enriched Max's life but also reinforced the trust and love between them.

For pets that are left alone for extended periods, providing mental stimulation and entertainment is crucial. Boredom can lead to destructive behavior or anxiety, so it's important to offer activities that keep your pet engaged. Puzzle toys, treat-dispensing devices, and interactive games can provide hours of entertainment and mental exercise. Emily discovered that Max enjoyed watching birds from the window, so she set up a bird feeder outside to create a dynamic and engaging view for him.

The physical environment also plays a significant role in your pet's comfort and happiness. Ensuring that your pet has access to cozy resting spots, whether it's a plush bed, a sunny windowsill, or a soft blanket, allows them to relax and recharge. Temperature control is another consideration, as pets can be sensitive to extreme heat or cold. Providing fans, heaters, or cooling mats can help maintain a comfortable climate for your pet.

In multi-pet households, creating a harmonious environment involves managing interactions between different animals. Introducing new pets should be done gradually and with care, allowing each animal to acclimate to the presence of the other. Providing separate resources, such as food bowls, litter boxes, and resting areas, can prevent competition and reduce tension. Emily was mindful of Max's territorial nature and ensured that he had his own space and resources, which helped maintain peace in her home.

Training and positive reinforcement are powerful tools in creating a loving environment. Teaching your pet basic commands or tricks not only enhances their safety but also strengthens your relationship. Positive reinforcement, such as treats or praise, encourages desired behaviors and fosters a sense of accomplishment in your pet. Emily found that Max responded well to clicker training, which provided mental stimulation and deepened their connection.

Finally, a loving environment is one where your pet's health and well-being are prioritized. Regular veterinary check-ups, a balanced diet, and proper grooming are essential components of responsible pet care. Monitoring your pet's health and addressing any concerns promptly ensures that they remain happy and healthy. Emily was diligent in scheduling routine vet visits for Max, ensuring that he received vaccinations, dental care, and any necessary treatments.

Creating a safe and loving environment is an ongoing commitment that evolves with your pet's needs and circumstances. By providing a secure, nurturing, and engaging home, you lay the foundation for a fulfilling and joyful life for your beloved companion. This environment not only enhances your pet's quality of life but also enriches your own, as the bond between you and your pet grows stronger with each passing day.